# THE REAL ENEMY OF ALL MANKIND

### PERRY ALAN PICKENS

PUBLISHED by PARABLES
Earthly Stories with a Heavenly Meaning

**The Real Enemy Of All Mankind**
Perry Alan Pickens

Published By Parables
October, 2021

All Rights Reserved. No part of this book may be reproduced or utilized in any form or by any means, electronic or mechanical, including photocopying, recording, or by any information storage and retrieval system, without permission in writing from the author.

Printed in the United States of America

Readers should be aware that Internet Web sites offered as citations and/or sources for further information may have been changed or disappeared between the time this was written and the time it is read.

# THE REAL ENEMY OF ALL MANKIND

## PERRY ALAN PICKENS

PUBLISHED by PARABLES
Earthly Stories with a Heavenly Meaning

## *Before I Begin:*

## Before I begin this work; I need to tell you this.

If you are reading this now, and have never accepted The Lord Jesus Christ as your Personal Savior, you are in Eternal Danger. You could die at any moment in your Sins. The Bible tells me in The Book of Ezekiel-more on that later-that if I fail to warn you of the Eternal Punishment for rejecting Christ, YOUR BLOOD WILL BE ON MY HANDS!

So, I'm taking the time to tell you now; how to avoid Hell Forever. Just Pray This Prayer:

> *"Lord Jesus. I'm a Sinner in need of Your Saving*

*Power. I Humble Myself before You, and confess that I need You to Save Me. I now ask You to Forgive Me of ALL MY SINS IN THOUGHT, WORD AND DEED, and ask you now to come into My Heart and My Life, and Save Me, because I cannot save myself from Hell. I now Thank You for coming into My Heart and My Life. Make Me Yours Lord. Amen!"*

There it is. I've warned you of what will happen if you reject Christ as Your Personal Savior. God Almighty will surely Reject You...from entrance into Heaven at Judgement Day!

The Real Enemy Of All Mankind

For My Only Daughter Trish;
and My Grandchildren: Tayana,
DeMarcus, Shardae, and My First
Great-Grandson. Ty Quinn...
And...

　　ALL THE REST OF HUMANITY

"Seek THE LORD. Above all else, and Cling TO HIM."

It will be The Best decision all of you will have EVER MADE!"

Perry Alan Pickens

The Real Enemy Of All Mankind

I.

Noah Webster: 1758-1843, is known as 'The Father of American Scholarship and Education.' He also held such Titles as Politician, Lawyer, Author, Schoolmaster and Newspaper Editor.

These are Two of his definitions of the term: 'Enemy'. I'll use the Third Definition first, as it is most applicable to the scope of this book.

Definition 3. In Theology and by way of eminence, The Enemy is The Devil. The Archfiend!

Definition 1. A Foe; an Adversary. A Private Enemy is One who hates another and wishes him/her* injury. A Public Enemy, or foe, is one who belongs to a nation or party, at war with another!


*=I added 'her', because The Enemy is out to get as many Women and Girls, as well as Men and Boys to share in his Eternal Fate of Hell along with him as possible.

The Real Enemy Of All Mankind

## II.

If you've ever seen the movie 'The Devil's Advocate', you'll most likely recall the scene toward the end, where Robert DeNiro's Character reveals his true self to Keanu Reeves' Character:

"Who are you?" Reeves.

"Ohh…I have so many names…" DeNiro.

The Author, and Producers got that one right. The Ku Klux Klan isn't my enemy or yours. The Proud Boys, Racist Police or Media Personalities aren't my enemy or yours. Radical Extremist Politicians are not your enemy or mine. Russia, China, North Korea, and all the Terrorist Organizations, and the Cartel, or Triads are not Our True Enemy. I could list many more groups. None of these nations and or groups are really Our Enemy.

You see; all of us Human Beings have One Enemy in common, and I can assure you of this: Inasmuch as you might believe you Hate Me, there is someone who hates YOU, far more than you will ever know. He is The True Source of all Hatred and Evil. I will endeavor to explain to you just who this being is. The only source of information I will use is God's Word. The Holy Bible. That is because it contains all the information about this adversary of Us All, that you'll ever need. I'll also use Google as well. You may or may not believe me, or even care. Yet, if you're still reading up to this point, I strongly urge you to continue on...for Your Sake!

This information WILL, give you cause to make the greatest choice you will ever make in your entire lifetime...and you DO have a choice to make when you reach the end of this book.

If, however you're already a Child of The King, keep reading!

Perry Alan Pickens

The Real Enemy Of All Mankind

## III.

Table of Contents:

Acknowledgements.

Part I. Defeated in Heaven.

1. Who Is THE Enemy?
2. His Origin.
3. His Objective.
4. The First War.
5. Why Hell Exists.

Part II. Defeated At Calvary.

6. The Demons.
7. Hard-Headed!
8. The Father of Lies.
9. The god of This World.

Part III. Defeated Forever!

10. The Last Days.
11. The Last War/Judgement!
12. A Final Word.
Last Call...and Choice!

The Real Enemy Of All Mankind

## Acknowledgements.

First and foremost; I give all Praise and honor to God Almighty, The Son Jesus Christ, and The Holy Spirit for keeping in my mind, the calling to write this book. I defer to The Great I AM, with any regard to any recognition I may receive upon review and critique of this work. All The Glory goes TO GOD. Not Me!

Second; I want to Thank My Late Parents: Jack Pickens Jr. Annie Mae Pickens, for raising me. My Siblings: Jackie, Joyce, Evonne, Marquita, Craig, Darryl and last but certainly not least, Stacy. My Elder Aunts: Aunt Jo, Aunt Neregie, Aunt Lola, Aunt Doris, Aunt Lillie Mae, and Aunt Mildred. My Elder Uncles: Uncle Bob, Uncle Johnny Jr. Uncle John, Uncle Clifford, Uncle Alfred. Uncle Myles-'Butch', and Uncle Charles-'Chuck'

Carter. All My Cousins and Extended Relatives too numerous to mention. They all know who they are as do I.

Every Pastor I've ever had and known in Life, and all Godly People the Good Lord put in my life to help in giving me sound, Godly Instruction although I rarely if ever paid attention to, or heeded it. I'm being honest about that too: The Late Rev. Wilkerson, Rev. Dillard, Rev. Robinson, Rev. Hornaday, Rev. Twillie. Still Living; Rev. Manson, all of Union Missionary Full Gospel Baptist Church in Burlington, Iowa. The Late Leonard Schantz, my former Music Teacher at BCHS. Mr. Richard W. Bundy of Greensburg, PA. Reverend Kevin Lee of Lifeways Ministries in Beaver Falls, PA. Minister Teddy Taylor, also of Lifeways Ministries. Rev. Validia Giddens, And finally; Don & Alice Johnston of Titus House Ministries in Albuquerque, NM. There are others,

## The Real Enemy Of All Mankind

and I hope I've not forgotten any of you either! If I have, I apologize.

Perry Alan Pickens

The Real Enemy Of All Mankind

# Part I.

# Defeated in Heaven.

Perry Alan Pickens

The Real Enemy Of All Mankind

## 1.

Who Is THE Enemy?

To know exactly who 'The Enemy' really is, I need to give you Scriptural Proof s that reveals who he is. They vary all throughout The Bible, but all point to the same person. The Lord Jesus illustrates this point about Satan, which stands out above all other definitions about him in The Gospel of John, while he argues with many of The Jews, about Spiritual Family Ties as opposed to Biological Ties. Chapter 8: vs. 37. New Geneva Study Bible, New King James Version. Jesus is speaking: "I know that you are Abraham's descendants, but you seek to kill Me, because My Word has no place in you." Now; The Jews decided to argue with Him in believing their Ancestry to Abraham justified them as Righteous, because of Biology. Jesus sets them straight in vs. 44: "You-The Jews claiming Abraham as their father-are of your father The Devil, and the desires of your father you want to do. He was a murderer from the beginning, and does not stand in the truth because there is no truth in him. When he speaks a lie, he speaks from his own resources, for he is a liar and the father of it..."

Satan is; The Father of Lies. If you've ever read in the Book of Genesis about Cain and his brother Abel, you already know that the first recorded murder in Biblical history took place. Abel was a keeper of Sheep. Cain was a tiller of the ground. The time had come for Offering in Worship to God, and Abel's was respected by God because he'd brought of The Firstborn to The Lord and their fat. I personally believe it was also because Abel had brought a Blood Sacrifice as well, to The Lord. Cain on the other hand; brought an offering of the fruit of the ground to The Lord...which God did not respect.

    Now, you might argue and say: "Well, Cain's should have been respected by God too." I believe it wasn't for this reason: Abel's Offering was also backed by Faith in God, despite his Parents' failure to obey Him because of The Fall.

    Cain's Offering was not backed by Faith in God, and he became angry because God didn't respect his Offering, and was tempted to Murder his own brother...which he subsequently did. I know...I know: "Well, The Devil Himself didn't kill Abel."

Perry Alan Pickens

## 2.

Consider this:

Have you ever been so angry at someone, that you said you could kill Him, Her, or It? I have in my own life. Jesus says in Matthew 5, vs. 21 & 22. "You have heard that it was said to those of old, You Shall Not Murder, and whoever Murders will be in danger of The Judgement. Vs. 22. "But I say to you, that whoever is angry with his brother WITHOUT A CAUSE shall be in danger of The Judgement..."

The Sin-and Crime-of Murder therefore, begins in The Heart, and the source of such sin, is ONLY, The Devil. The Father of Lies! You may wonder as I have, just how The Devil came into existence in the first place. All Things Considered.

The first of two answers I've found; is in the Book of Isaiah. Chapter 14, starting in verse 12:

"How you are fallen from Heaven O Lucifer, son of the morning. How you are cut down to the ground. You who weakened the nations." Vs. 13. "For you have said in your heart: I will ascend into Heaven, I will exalt my throne above the stars of God; I will also sit on the mount of the congregation on the farthest sides of the north. Vs. 14. I will ascend above the heights of the clouds; I will be like the Most-High."

Vs: 15-20 I believe, tell of his great misfortune and downfall. Later on, I will go into detail, as to how this transpired according to Scripture. Again, I'll be relying on God's Word alone for this. Nothing else will or can, do!

## The Real Enemy Of All Mankind

The first mistake Lucifer made; was to allow The Sin of Pride to enter and become firmly entrenched in his entire being. He had it made. He was one who had High Prominence in Heaven among the Angels. All he had to do, was just be satisfied with his position that he had.

But Nooooooo. He couldn't do that.

He just had to try and take over Heaven. He tried doing it literally by force. That didn't work out so well for him as you will see later on.

Perry Alan Pickens

## 3.

His Origin.

As I'd alluded to earlier; I'd said that I would tell you how he-The Devil-came into being. First however, you need to know this about the Bible: It is called; The Holy Bible, because it's true Author-God Almighty-is Holy. It is a Sacred Book because if transcends, and stands apart and above, every other book ever written. It always will. It is even higher than this one. That is why I trust only God's Word alone, and nothing else!

Let's get some things straight right off the bat about The Devil.

First; Satan is a Created Being-for he was at first the Angel Lucifer-and has Superhuman Abilities. However, he is NOT Divine. Second;

he possesses much in the way of knowledge and power but, he is NOT Omniscient, Omnipresent, or Omnipotent. In short, he cannot know All Things. Only God Alone is Omniscient, and only He has that right to do so. Third; Satan cannot be everywhere all at once. That is why he has Demons on his side. He sends them out to constantly bother, harass and when possible, directly infect and possess anyone willing to open themselves up to Evil Influence. God on the other hand, CAN be everywhere at once, because not only is He truly Divine, but He also has the power to be everywhere at the same exact time. Fourth; and finally; Satan is not All Powerful. Recall that I'd just told you that he was created. Therefore, he CANNOT possess All Power in the first place. He has no more power than what God allows him to have.

## The Real Enemy Of All Mankind

As such; you and I don't have to be outright afraid of him, and we don't have to live in terror of him or his Demons. Here's why: The Lord Jesus has already BEATEN HIM, at The Cross! Now, Satan wants you to disbelieve everything you just read. In fact, I'm not surprised that right now, he's telling you: 'Look, this dude doesn't know what he's talking about and he isn't all that great a person himself. Why not get rid of this book. You don't need to read any more of this, messed-up bunk!'

One last thing: I used to believe that Satan could read my mind. I know better today. You see; he only hears What You Say. He cannot know What You Think. Only God Almighty can do that, for He created your very Brain, as He did with mine. So, only He knows just how it works!

Perry Alan Pickens

## 4.

His Objective.

I don't have to go into a lot of detail about Satan's Plans for you and I. They're pretty straightforward. He knows what his ultimate end will be. So, as I'd said earlier, he wants to take as many of us into Hell and The Lake of Fire with him and his Demonic Forces, as possible. It's not his nature to do or be anything close to Benevolent. It never has been and it never will. He knows his time in short, and he'll do everything in his power to ensure he gets some kind of 'fantasy, hoped-for-win,' over God in the final battle to take place. I'll tell you more on that also much later on.

It is his intention, to give everyone the impression that everything is hopeless and that we should just live any way we want to.

That after we die, that's it. There's no Hell. No Heaven. Only Nothing. Well, NOTHING could be further from The Truth. Case in Point: Hebrews 9:27. "And as it is appointed for men to die once, but after this The Judgement."

You, Me and Every Human Soul that ever has, currently is living, or ever will be born, WILL face God Almighty at the time of Judgement. I'll say more on this later on in the book. So don't believe The Hype that when you die, it's all over. It Isn't, not by a long shot. You see, EVERYONE, WILL HAVE AN ETERNAL DESTINY. It's going to be one of two places: Heaven, or Hell. There is no Getting Around this. No Escape from this. No Bargaining One's Way Out of This. No Nothing! The Devil already knows this. So, it's his Objective to ensure he gets as many Co-Sufferers along with him into The Lake of Fire, as possible. It's like the Old Saying: 'If I got to go, I'm going to take you with me!' Rest assured, he is relentless and will never stop trying to dissuade you from Your Faith in Christ if you're Saved. He'll try any and everything he can, to make you think you've lost your Salvation even after accepting Christ as Lord and Savior. I know, because I used to think that because of My Sins...and Antisocial Behaviors that used to get me into all kinds of trouble over and again!

Here's The Truth: Once you accept Christ as Savior, the only way you lose Salvation IS IF YOU DIE, WHILE STILL SINNING! Proof: Hebrews again. Chapter 10: vs. 26-31. Get a Load of This:

Perry Alan Pickens

5.

Hebrews 10: vs. 26. "For if we sin willfully after we have received the Knowledge of the Truth, there no longer remains a sacrifice for sins." Vs. 27. "But a certain fearful expectation of Judgement and Fiery Indignation which will devour the adversaries." {That is, The Devil and ALL his Demons.} Vs. 28. "Anyone who has rejected Moses' law, dies without mercy on the testimony of two or three witnesses." Vs. 29. "Of how much Worse Punishment, do you suppose, will he be thought worthy who has trampled The Son of God underfoot, counted the Blood of the Covenant by which he was Sanctified a common thing, and insulted the Spirit of Grace?" Vs. 30. "For we know Him who said, 'Vengeance is Mine. I will repay' says The Lord." And again: "The Lord WILL Judge His

People." Vs. 31. "It is a fearful thing, to fall into the hands of The Living God!"

In short, you'd have to be utterly Foolish, to think along these lines:

'Well, I know I'll get forgiveness after I do this or that. I'll just pray for forgiveness after I...' Now I used to do that on a constant basis, until my Elder Sister Marquita told me: "You CAN have your Name Erased from The Book of Life Perry."

I did some checking on my own, and found out in the Scriptures- particularly those I just quoted from The Word of God-that I'd have to literally CONTINUE LIVING THE WAY I USED TO AND THEN DIE WHILE LIVING A SINFUL, SELF-CENTERED LIFE OUTSIDE OF THE GRACE OF GOD! It's ONLY <u>after</u> Physical Death, that such a punishment would be certain, however, while still alive, there IS a way back to Grace. It's found here: 1 John: 1: vs.8-10: Vs 8." If we say we have no sin, we deceive ourselves, and the Truth is not in us." Vs. 9: "If we Confess Our Sins, He-Jesus-is Faithful and Just to forgive us our sins <u>and to cleanse us</u> FROM ALL UNRIGHTEOUSNESS." Vs. 10: "If we say we have not sinned, we make Him a liar, and His Word is not in us!" Let's also consider The Apostle Paul from the Book of Romans in Chapter 7: Vs. 15-25. First, a little Backstory about him.

He was originally; Saul, and a former Pharisee who had the reputation of persecuting Christian Believers. In Chapter 8 of the Book of Acts; Saul is actively attempting to destroy and eradicate the Early Church, and entering houses to drag off men and women to prison identified as Early Church Believers.

Perry Alan Pickens

## 6.

Take note however; of how God uses even this disturbance, to work {'Everything to Good', to those who love The Lord, even to The Called According to His Purpose.} That, is Romans; Chapter 8: Vs. 28. You see, in persecuting the early Church, Saul was actually helping to Spread the Gospel. According to Acts Chapter 8, Vs. 1. A fellow named Philip, also preaching Christ, went to Samaria. Casting out Demonic Possessed People, and healing Paralyzed People so they could walk and run again! Man, was there A LOT of happy people. Saul however; was not satisfied, and was still attacking the Early Church...until the Road to Damascus. The Lord lit up Saul with Light from Heaven, and knocked him to the ground asking why he was persecuting the Church...the very Body of Christ. Acts 9: Vs. 4. 'Then he fell to the ground, and heard a voice saying to him.' "Saul, Saul, why are you persecuting Me?" Vs. 5. And he-Saul- said, 'Who are you Lord? ' Then The Lord said: "I am Jesus, whom you are persecuting. It is hard for you to kick against the goads." Vs. 6. So, he, trembling and astonished said: "Lord, what do you want me to do?" Vs. 6. "Arise and go into the city, and you will be told what you must do." His men accompanying him, had to lead him along.

    And so it began. For three days, Saul would not have his sight back, but is sent to a guy named Ananias who subsequently prayed for him, and the scales of blindness fell from his eyes. Eventually, his name would be changed from Saul, to Paul.

## The Real Enemy Of All Mankind

It wasn't long after, I would imagine, that he also found out this particular truth of living The Christian Life here on Earth now, and it is found in the letter to The Romans. Chapter7: Vs.19-25. "For the good that I will to do, I do not do, but the evil I will not to do, that I practice." Vs. 20. "Now if I do what I will not to do, it is no longer I who do it but sin that dwells in me." Vs. 21. "I find then a law, that evil is present with me, the one who wills to do good." Vs.22. "For I delight in the Law of God according to the inward man." Vs. 23. "But I see another law in my members warring against the law of my mind, and bringing me into captivity to the law of sin which is in my members." Vs. 24. "O wretched man that I am! Who will deliver me from this body of death?" Vs. 25. "I Thank God-through Jesus Christ Our Lord!"

The Apostle Paul is able to sum it all up like this:

Perry Alan Pickens

## 7.

Even for Christian Believers; indwelling sin is and will still be a problem, because it's based in Our Flesh. You remember that Old School Song from back in the day: 'Do It, Till You're Satisfied?' Most of you don't, unless you're the same age as I or close to it. Yet, you recall the Lyrics: "Everybody knows, what they like to do. Whatever it is, do it. Long as it pleases you. Just take some time, and relax your mind, and do it. Do it. Do it till you're satisfied!"

Well, that formula won't work for Us as Believers in Christ. Here's why: We are called to 'Resist the Devil and he will flee from you.' The only way to successfully do so, is to utilize the Indwelling Power of The Holy Spirit that Jesus places in Us when we accept Him as Lord and

Savior...and CHOOSING TO DO SO DAILY! Indwelling sin is temporary, and when Jesus comes for his Church, we will be changed from Corruptible to Incorruptible. In short, the indwelling sin will be eradicated from us when He comes to literally Re-Make Us all over again! He will take the sin nature OUT of Us for all Eternity when he gives us new Bodies and Minds.

Hallelujah!

I attend a Monthly Meeting called 'Circle of Concern' over The Internet, and it's with a group of Fellow Believers from all over the country and planet. We even have a member from the United Kingdom. We discuss our common struggles in maintaining our Walk with Christ, and we pray for one another, help uplift one another, and rejoice with one another when Good Things happen to any of us. The one thing we remind ourselves over and again every month, is that we DO NOT, ever have to willfully return to our Old Way of living. Doing so, brings absolutely NOTHING but Misery, Heartache, and Constant Sorrow. We recall that Jesus said this too. John's Gospel. Chapter 16: Vs. 33. "These things I have spoken to you, that in Me, you may have peace. In the world, you will have tribulation, but be of good cheer. I HAVE OVERCOME THE WORLD!"

This is why I as a Believer, have not just hope, but I have a Blessed Hope...because of The Lord, Jesus Christ!

Perry Alan Pickens

8.

The First War.

Believe it or not; the very first war to have ever been fought, didn't take place here on Earth. It took place in Heaven. I'd given you the reference with regard to the Book of Isaiah, 14: 12-17. Yet, there is another in the Book of Ezekiel, Chapter 28: Vs. 12-17 also. Now for clarification, in Ezekiel, God is telling the Prophet, and referring to him as 'Son of Man' to make this particular Lamentation against the King of Tyre. Apparently; it was some type of city that possessed a kind of Island Fortress. Another King named Nebuchadnezzar, from the Kingdom of Babylon, attacked it in 585 B.C. Yet, the Island Fortress part of it remained for another thirteen years until 572 B. C. Apparently; The King of Tyre wanted the Trade Routes that Jerusalem had previously controlled, and because of Jerusalem's loss of the routes, the King of Tyre-I believe- became intoxicated with joy over Jerusalem's fall and demise. Well, God had an answer for that too...by introducing the Kingdom of Babylon against it. In a way; this would also be alluded to the Fall of Lucifer as well, and starting in verse 15 of the Book of Ezekiel 28, we read this: "You were perfect in your ways from the day you were created. Till Iniquity was found in you." Vs. 16. "By the abundance of your Trading, you became filled with violence within, and you sinned. Therefore, I cast you as a profane thing out of the mountain of God and I destroyed you, O Covering Cherub, from the midst of the fiery stones." Vs. 17. "Your heart was lifted up because of your beauty. You corrupted your wisdom for the sake of your splendor.

## The Real Enemy Of All Mankind

I cast you to the ground. I laid you before kings, that they might gaze at you." It might be said that the phrase: "By the abundance of your trading..." could infer that Lucifer used a promise of shared spoils of Heaven, with many of the Angels. Like Us Human Beings, they too were under a period of 'Divine Probation' as it were at first. So, it stands to reason then, that God already knew what was coming with regard to Lucifer's plans anyway and had a plan of His own, to counter and defeat them. Nothing catches God by surprise. Moreover; there are 9 different types of Angels, and they have a Hierarchy among them as well. They go in this order: 1 Seraphim. Isaiah. 6: 1-7. They are known as 'The Burning Ones'. They also are Attendants at The Throne of God and Praise Him Constantly. They have Six Wings. Two to cover their face. Two to cover their feet, and two to fly. 2. Cherubim. Exodus. 25: 18-21, Ezekiel. 10-14, and Revelation. 4-

6. The rest are: 'Thrones', 'Dominions', 'Virtues'. 'Powers', 'Principalities', 'Archangels', and 'Angels'!

## 9.

Lucifer's Former Function; was to simply serve the Will of God, and to continually praise Him. Lucifer as being an Angel of the second highest order of the ninefold celestial hierarchy, also was bigger than most of the other Angels and I would imagine, appeared quite intimidating. Because he decided that because of his attributes given him by God- remember that he was created as well-made him as fit to rule in Heaven as opposed to God Himself, the Sin of Pride crept into his very being.

The Five 'I Wills', then formed in his mind and he made his choice. He began recruiting many other Angels to follow along with him and once he'd decided he had enough, he made his move and began The First Mutiny and War.

Like I said earlier however; nothing catches God by surprise, and He had the rest of the faithful remaining Angelic Host fight along with Him-I can see Jesus in the battle too-and ultimately, Lucifer and his group, LOST!

Thus, God created Hell. It is deep in The Earth itself, and I would imagine it is quite close to the Core of the Planet. It is the place where all Evil and Wicked Beings are sent. Lucifer-now named Satan-was cast down there along with his now Demonic Attendees. However; Satan still managed to infuse himself into the affairs of Adam and Eve, by causing Eve to first taste the Forbidden Fruit of The Tree of The Knowledge of Good & Evil. When she offered some of it to her husband Adam, I can see Satan waiting behind some bush or tree saying to himself:

## The Real Enemy Of All Mankind

'Come on. Do it. Just one Bite, and I'll Have You and All Humanity!' Well, when Adam also ate, that's when Satan Officially became: The god of this world!

Adam was created first. So, the Spiritual Responsibility of Relationship to The Creator was on him...not Eve. By choosing to eat the Forbidden Fruit, he chose to become a Rebel against God and His Divine Word...and as a result, cursed not only he and Eve, but ALL MANKIND! You and I, as the Decedents of the first Human Beings on Earth, also share in carrying this same curse known as Sin! Still, God had another plan for Us. He let Satan know about it as well:

Genesis 3: 14 &15. Gives the account of what is to transpire not only for the Creature Serpent and its Kind, but also for the future of Satan and the coming battles yet to take place. God addresses Satan directly now: Vs. 14.

Perry Alan Pickens

10.

So, The Lord God said to the Serpent: "Because you have done this, you are cursed more than all cattle and more than every beast of the field. On your belly you shall go, and you shall eat dust all the days of your life." Vs. 15. "And, I will put enmity between you and the woman, and between your seed and her Seed. He shall bruise your head, and you shall bruise His Heel."

So, now God resets the stage for what would happen from that very day forth, all the way to now and ultimately The End. First; he converts the depravation of the woman's affections from Satan to Himself. Hence, the 'Enmity'. The Dictionary defines the Noun, as this: 'The State or feeling of being actively opposed to someone or something.' With regard to Eve, She and all

Humans to come, would now have a deep-seeded dislike or ill will towards any and all serpents...or snakes. It is derived from the Anglo-French Word which, while not quite the same, still has the qualities of being an-Wait for It-Enemy! As for the phrase: '...Your seed and Her Seed...' Humanity is now divided into two communities: The Redeemed, who love God, and the reprobate, who love Self. The Division is expressed quickly, when Cain murders his brother Abel. Yet, in the Future, The Prophecy will and ultimately does find fulfillment, when Jesus Christ comes later on, and dies on The Cross and Rises from The Grave. This is why He is also known as 'The Second Adam'. This is because He has united The Redeemed with Him, over the forces of Sin, Death and the Devil. Christ had to suffer, in order to serve the Higher Purpose of winning the New Community-Redeemed-from the dominion of the god of this world-the

## The Real Enemy Of All Mankind

Serpent's by shedding his own Blood on the Cross and rising from the Grave to defeat Death itself. There's a Part II coming: When Christ appears at His Second Coming-2$^{nd}$ Thessalonians 1: 5-10, and also in the same book: Chapter 2: Vs. 1-4. More on these will come later. So, in conclusion: Round I Score: God-1. Satan-0. You would think that at that moment in time, he'd just give up, right? WRONG. Now Satan is vexed, and now decides to turn ALL his attention squarely on ALL HUMANITY, which includes You and Me. He still hates God mind you, but now more than ever, he has designs on taking as many of Us to his Final Destination-Hell-along with him as possible. Satan is relentless, and that is why he never tires: "From going to and fro, on the earth, and from walking back and forth on it." Job: Chapter 1. Vs.7.

Perry Alan Pickens

## 11.

Why Hell Exists.

I've heard this question periodically in my life: 'Why would a Loving God, create such a terrible place as Hell, and send people there that refuse to live the way He wants us to?' It is the final destination for everyone condemned to eternal punishment at The Last Judgement. Matthew 25: 41-46. Revelation 20: 11-15. It is a place of Fire and Darkness. Jude 7 & 13. Weeping and Gnashing of Teeth. Matthew 8: 12, 13: 42, & 50, 22: 13, 24: 51, 25: 30. Destruction. 2nd Thessalonians 1: 7-9, 2nd Peter 3: 7 1st Thessalonians 5: 3 and Torment. Revelation 20: 10, Luke 16: 23. Make no mistake about this. God intended for it to be the final destination strictly for Satan and his Demonic Horde, but God is Holy. He cannot and WILL NOT, allow sin OF

ANY TYPE, to be in Heaven with Him and the Saints. It is something to literally take seriously people...for real! Just as Heaven is as Wonderful, Beautiful and Peaceful more than we could ever imagine or know. Hell is as Terrible, Horrifying, and Far Worse than what we could ever imagine or dream up. There is no Horror Script or Movie, that can ever come close to detailing the absolute reality of Hell, in existence. There have been instances however; where some people have died, and for a brief period of time, experienced Hell. The Lord brought them back, just so they could warn others and the rest of us of its reality and certainty.

Moreover; Hell is not just the total absence of God, but it is also the Final Consequence of His Wrath. If you die and end up there, it is because YOU, chose to live for yourself and the pleasures of this world, indulging in whatever sin or sins you love. YOU, rejected The Creator. The Lord who made you and made a way for you to be Saved and be in Heaven with Him. Now Mind You; there also are people who have died, and gone to Heaven for a brief period of time as God allowed, so they could see for themselves just what it is like. Then, they were sent back to earth and revived in their bodies again. Everyone that's experienced this, has a slightly different story on what they saw, but one thing is common to all: Perfect Peace & Happiness! I'll say that again: Perfect Peace & Happiness!

That, is what I want when it's time for this body to return to the dust.

Perry Alan Pickens

The Real Enemy Of All Mankind

# Part II.

# Defeated At Calvary.

Perry Alan Pickens

## 12.

### The Demons.

The word 'Demon' or 'devil' as some translations tell them. Come from the Greek 'daimon', or 'daimonion'. In any case; they are fallen angels, and creatures that cannot die, and serve Satan. Matthew 12: 24-29. Vs. 24: Now when the Pharisees heard it-the casting out report-they said: "This fellow does not cast out demons except by 'Beelzebub'-Satan-the ruler of the demons." Vs. 25: But Jesus knew their thoughts, and said to them: "Every kingdom divided against itself is brought to desolation, and every city or house divided against itself will not stand." Vs. 26: "If Satan casts out Satan, he is divided against himself.

How then, will his kingdom stand?" Vs. 27: "And if I cast out demons by Beelzebub, by whom do your sons cast <u>them</u> out? Therefore, they shall be your judges." Vs. 28: "But if I cast out demons by the Spirit of God, surely the Kingdom of God has come upon you." Vs. 29: "Or how can one enter a strong man's house and plunder his goods, unless he first binds the strong man? And then he will plunder his house." Jesus illustrated further on, that anyone not aligned with Him, with regard to the Spiritual Warfare we as Believers MUST FIGHT, is thus, AGAINST HIM!

Satan Worshippers; please take heed to what I'm about to tell you. The Devil DOESN'T CARE ABOUT YOU. HE STILL HATES YOU, and so also does his Demonic Horde. You're claiming allegiance to him, is only doing nothing but sealing your doom upon your physical body's death without being saved by Jesus Christ!

## The Real Enemy Of All Mankind

The demons-if you allow their influence into your body and mind-WILL DESTROY YOU! They have various means at their disposal to do so too.

You've seen the movie 'The Exorcist', and other demonic-possession flicks like it right? Well, THE REALITY IS FAR, FAR WORSE! If you play with any type of items of divination-like Ouija Boards-you are literally playing with fire...HELL FIRE! Demons will wait for you to try using such things to enter into your very being. Once they do-and they always come in packs like wolves-THEY GOT YOU! Oh, it might be just one at first, but not long after, he's bringing in the rest of the Pack.

I had a rather frightening situation happen to me twice in my life:

Perry Alan Pickens

## 13.

I woke up at my Parents' House when I was a teenager in my bedroom, and I could not move. I was fully awake and aware, but it felt like something HEAVY was sitting on my chest, and I could hardly breathe. I struggled to move, but I couldn't even more my little finger. Not knowing what else to do, I started calling out The Name of Jesus in my mind, and within seconds, that pressure was just as suddenly lifted from me and I got up. I told no one about this. Not even My Family knows-until now that is-because back then, I didn't think anyone would believe me. The same thing happened again many years later too...in an apartment I was renting and I'd been living alone then. I called on the Name of Jesus in my mind again, and I was freed again.

They have knowledge and strength. They inflict or exploit mental maladies and physical ones too. They also use deception and discouragement in a variety of forms. Most especially, against Believers in Christ having the indwelling of the Holy Spirit. However; they cannot deter God's Final Purpose of saving His Elect. Just as they cannot escape their impending torment to come. Christ has given Us Believers the ability to also cast out demons in His Name, because it is by His Power. Now to be sure, it also takes a serious effort in prayer before attempting to do so. If one is not careful, it CAN backfire and then there's serious consequences that are as bad if not outright worse. Case in point. Acts 19: 11-16. Vs. 11. Now God, worked unusual miracles by the hands of Paul, Vs. 12 so that even handkerchiefs or aprons were brought from his body to the sick, and the diseases left them and the evil spirits went out of them. Vs. 13. Then some of the Itinerant-Traveling-Jewish Exorcists took it upon themselves, to call on the Name of The Lord Jesus over those who had evil spirits, saying: "We exorcise you, by the Jesus whom Paul preaches." Vs. 14. Also, there were seven sons of Sceva, a Jewish Chief Priest, who did so. {Now, this is where it all goes bad:} Vs. 15 And the evil spirit answered and said "Jesus I know, and Paul I know; but who are you?" Vs. 16. Then, the man in whom the evil spirit was, leaped on them, overpowered them, and prevailed against them, so that they fled out of that house naked and wounded.

If you're going to cast out Demons in the Name of Jesus; you'd better first be Saved and Filled with The Holy Ghost, and be Prayed-Up,

Ready to do Spiritual Battle. <u>THIS IS NO JOKE AT ALL! THIS IS SERIOUS BUSINESS!!</u>

## 14.

Hard-Headed!

When I was a youngster, my mother, would periodically tell me that I was acting or being 'Hard-Headed'. I'd hear that, especially when it came to doing something I was supposed to do and I knew I was supposed to do it, but still didn't or resisted doing it. Other names of the same behavior are: 'Stubborn', 'Unyielding', or even 'Stiff-Necked'. Mom would also tell me that, a Hard Head would make a Soft Behind or Buttocks. Hence, The Whippings.

Sin is exactly that. The Devil is a master of being Hard-Headed, and he consistently tries over and again, to get as many of Us Human Beings to act like he does. It's one way he ensures his mission objective: John's Gospel 10: Vs. 10. Jesus is speaking to the Disciples during another training session: Vs. 10. "The Thief does not come except to steal, and to kill, and to destroy. I have come that they-We the Redeemed-may have life, and that they may have it more abundantly!" The Life that Jesus gives is truly unique from any other concept of life, in that it is Eternal and moreover, He gives it in abundance to those of Us that respond to His Call for Salvation through accepting Him as Lord and Savior, and Believing in Him and His Sacrifice on the Cross for Us as well as His Rising from The Dead, and living for Him!

The Devil and his Demonic Horde on the other hand, DON'T, want you knowing or believing in this, because it cuts short his objective. That's why they constantly come at Us through our minds. Recall that I said, the devil Cannot read your mind. He can only hear what you say.

He acts on whatever you say, to begin his attack on you. Here's an illustration I'll use from my own life: I'm at Walmart doing some grocery shopping, and notice a young and attractive woman walking just ahead of me with her husband. She's wearing very revealing clothing and I say to one of my friends with me: "Man, I should be her husband. I'd Hit That Day and Night!" Instantly, a thought comes into my mind and it's one that I begin mentally undressing her to engage in sex with her. I just committed Adultery.

    To make matters worse, her husband notices and gives me an extreme look of warning that tell me: 'BACK OFF. THAT'S MY WIFE!' It is certainly not friendly either, or, he just might come out and say it to me directly.

He has every right to say what he ultimately said to me, and I had absolutely no right to look at his wife in the fashion I know, he recognized. Men know when other men take notice of their wives or girlfriends in lustful manners. That's also known as 'Covetousness'. It too, is a sin that God told Us we should never engage in. Exodus 20: 17. God Himself is giving His Ten Commandments to Moses at Mount Sinai, and this is one of them: Vs. 17. "You shall not covet your neighbor's house; you shall not covet your neighbor's wife, nor his male servant, nor his female servant, nor his ox, nor his donkey, <u>nor anything that is your neighbor's!</u>"

This is what the word 'Covet' means: 'To yearn to possess something.'

Satan will use Covetousness; as the sin by which the crimes of Theft, Murder, Assault-and yes this includes Sexual Assault- occur. It is about Self-Gratification despite what the Husband, Owner, Boyfriend, Parent, Sister, Brother, Wife, Child, Work Supervisor, even your Best Friend, feel about you engaging in it with someone whom they love or something they own.

I was guilty of this sin MANY times over in my life, and sometimes even to this day, I have to constantly watch what I think and say, so I give the Enemy as few chances to tempt me as possible with this kind of sin or any other for that matter. To be sure, he's coming FOR YOU TOO, IN THE EXACT SAME FASHION!

Here's something else to consider too. People often say things along these lines: "Man, I couldn't help it. I had to do it." "I mean, it was right there, what else was I supposed to do?" "I'm not hurting anybody, so no one will know anyway." Etcetera. These types of rationalizations come straight from the very pits of Hell itself. This is

Satan's methodology of thought-reversal, such that we become convinced that wrong is right...and somehow, right ends up being wrong. James 3: 13-18, show just how to know what is Heavenly Wisdom, Vs. Demonic Wisdom. James is speaking: Vs. 13. "Who is wise and understanding among you? Let him show by good conduct that his works-deeds-are done in the meekness of wisdom." Vs. 14. "But if you have bitter envy and self-seeking in your hearts, do not boast and lie against the Truth."

16.

Vs. 15. "This wisdom DOES NOT descend from above, but is earthly, sensual, Demonic." Vs. 16. "For where envy and self-seeking exist, confusion and every evil thing ARE THERE." Vs. 17. "But the wisdom that is from above is first, pure, then peaceable, gentle, willing to yield, full of mercy and good fruits, without partiality and without hypocrisy." Vs. 18. "Now the fruit of righteousness is sown in peace, by those who make peace." We also see in this same Epistle, the following admonition as well. Chapter 4: Vs. 7. "Therefore, submit to God. Resist the devil and he will flee from you." You might ask: "How is this possible?" by utilizing what The Scripture calls: 'The Whole Armor of God'. In essence, it is Our Spiritual Combat Suit and the way to

'Suit Up' is found in the Epistle of Ephesians Chapter 6. Vs. 11-18. You want to know how to beat up on the devil, instead of him and his demons beating up on and constantly mentally assaulting you? Your answers are: The Helmet of Salvation. The Breastplate of Righteousness. The Preparation of The Gospel of Peace. The Shield of Faith. Girded Waist with The Truth. The Sword of The Spirit. God's Word, and CONSTANT PRAYER! Remember; Satan is Hard-Headed. He cannot and WILL NOT, ever give up on attacking you, me or any of the rest of the Human Race. It is kind of like the Narrator in the GEICO Commercial. You know how he'd sound:

'When You're the Devil, you keep tempting people to Sin. It's what you do!' That's EXACTLY, what Satan does. It's his Specialty. He is a Master Deceiver. He'll use any and every trick in and out of any other book on

## The Real Enemy Of All Mankind

the planet-except God's Word-to try and get your mind off of the Lord, and onto other things. If he can distract and harass you into worrying and fretting about everything wrong in the world, then you're not seeking the One who is the Solution to overcoming the World. The Lord Jesus Christ! The Devil will NEVER give up on trying to get you or me. He's Insane. He's truly the Hardest, of Hard-Headed Beings to ever be in existence. There are times I wish that God would wipe him out completely.

However; Satan's Demise is not in My Time. It is in God's Time. So, until then, my job is like the Old Spiritual my grandmother used to sing: 'Well, I'm on the Battlefield, for My Lord. Yes, I'm on, the Battlefield, for My Lord. Well, I promised Him that I, would serve Him 'till I die. Yes, I'm on, the Battlefield, for My Lord!' Time to Suit-Up!!

Perry Alan Pickens

17.

The Father of Lies.

One of the reasons Jesus gave the Devil this kind of title; is because one of his missions is to invade Churches, and use those dedicated to him, to assist in its destruction. The Apostle Paul reveals this in 2nd Corinthians 11: Vs. 13-15. Vs. 13. "For such are false apostles, deceitful workers, transforming themselves into apostles of Christ." Vs. 14. "And No Wonder! For Satan himself transforms himself into an angel of light." Vs. 15 "Therefore it is no great thing if his ministers also transform themselves into ministers of righteousness, whose end will be according to their works." When Houses of Worship are disrupted by a few members within it, nothing short of total chaos ensues. I saw this once firsthand as a boy, at one of the church meetings I used to go to with my mom. I can't recall if it was Prayer Meeting or not, but arguments broke out. I cannot recall either, what it was all about. I Do Recall however; being quite shocked over the entire affair.

One thing ended up being certain; we lost a Pastor and his entire family, and it would be a few months, before we were blessed with another Pastor. He was one of the Men of God, who would begin helping to shape my Spiritual Growth. I would witness no more arguments within the Church from that point on. As a soon-to-be teenager, I began finding out exactly why Gossiping-actually another form of sin-was rampant, even in my Church. Envy gives Gossip energy to function. When people spend hours on the telephone talking about someone else-or a few of them-sooner or later, such conversations are bound to include many negatives about the same person or people. Envy looks at the kind of car he or she drives. The kind of job he or she has. The kind of house he or she lives in, and of course, the kinds of clothes he or she wears AT Sunday Service! One of the most powerful weapons the Devil uses all the time, is Sex. There was a lady I knew from our Church as a youngster, who dressed in rather revealing outfits. I won't mention her name, but my mom used to warn me about having anything to do with her. It was said that; she delved into Occult practices, for the purpose of luring young men-and daring teenage boys-into sexual escapades with her at secret hours of the night or occasions during the day on weekends. I'll be honest about this too: I wanted her. She had a most voluptuous body, and she knew I wanted her. She openly participated in Worship though.

Perry Alan Pickens

18.

There are to be sure, other things the Devil uses to try keeping us from Christ. I ought to know; because, I was heavy into drug use-including alcohol consumption-during my teenage and young adult years. I'd heard the phrase; 'Sex, Drugs, & Rock & Roll' often. I'd replaced the latter with 'Funk' instead. The music I'd listened to at the time, often encouraged openly rebelling against established moral norms. I'd mentioned one song from earlier if you recall: 'Do it Till You're Satisfied'. You can well imagine what 'It' is, that the title refers to, and it could be just about anything that promotes Self-Indulgence or some form of Self-Gratification.

The thing about such behaviors though, is that as pleasurable as they are at first, they become part of you and ultimately hurt you later in life. The parallel to this comes from Proverbs 20: Vs. 1. "Wine is a mocker. Strong drink is a brawler, and whoever is led astray by it, is not wise." Many a time, I drank way too much Mad Dog 20-20, Pabst Blue Ribbon, Schlitz, Budweiser, and a plethora of varying Hard Liquors. Add to that; Weed, Pills, Hallucinogens, and Chemicals like Paint Thinners for 'Huffing'-taking in the vapors for a 'High'-and you've got the perfect recipe for Overdose and Death! There was a time during my teenage years, I'd become depressed with life because I wasn't getting the same attention as my Older Brothers were from the Girls and Women. I decided I'd had enough of living and wanted out.

The Real Enemy Of All Mankind

God however, had other plans for me and spared me. That wasn't the first time either. I can say with 1000% Truth, that The Lord has rescued me from Death, time and again: Attempted Overdoses, Car Accidents, Potentially Being Shot, Brutal Traumatic Assaults, Sickness, Drowning, and even Dangerously Murderous Environments, as well as People!

You can't tell me there is no God, and expect me to believe it.

Satan however, will try and tell <u>You</u> though. Another trick he uses, is using Science itself, to deceive us all.

Take the Coronavirus Pandemic. Time and again, not only our government-in the Administration prior to the present one-for the most part, DID NOT heed the warnings of Health Specialists and Professionals, about the danger of not Masking and Social Distancing. The importance of

Perry Alan Pickens

Vaccination, now that it is available,
is yet something most people avoid.

## 19.

Although many, have had some type of adverse reaction to one of the various types of Vaccines available, just as many others if not more, have not had any at all. Yet, the Devil hears people's fears about them, and tell them lies like these: 'It isn't safe.' 'You don't need the Vaccine.' 'It will make you sick and/or kill you'. 'They didn't test it long enough, and hurried making it'. In the end, if you don't bother with finding out enough information for yourself about the Vaccine, chances are you have or will avoid getting it. All because, you heeded The Father of Lies! I love this retort whenever I hear it: 'Look man, my sister got it and got sick. She said don't get the shot'. 'My Co-Workers got the shot, and half of them are still sick from it at home. They were just fine before they got it.' The reasoning goes on and on.

Meanwhile, nearly everyone seemed to have forgotten that, better than 500,000 people in the United States alone-never mind the rest of the Planet-DIED from this Renegade Virus in almost the past two years! COVID-19 by the way, isn't the only Virus that's come up over the past 20-30 years to have tried taking out Humanity, and as these are The Last Days, Scripture proves it. Jesus says in Matthew 24: 7-8. "For nation will rise against nation, and kingdom against kingdom. And there will be famines, pestilences-DISEASES-and earthquakes in various places." Vs. 8. "All these are THE BEGINNING OF SORROWS!"

Nations are at odds with each other more and more, and the U.S. is

## The Real Enemy Of All Mankind

not exempt. We've got potential trouble with Russia, China, North Korea, and let's not forget Terrorist Organizations like ISIS too. We hear of Famine nearly all the time somewhere on the Planet. When was the last time you heard of the frequency of earthquakes being more than just one or two every year? I'm thinking the answer is: Never. Yet; life continues going on as if everything's okay, and people are living out there lives as usual. Still, the Signs of The Times are more and more evident: Government Capitol Riots over Elections. Unwarranted Police Shootings of People of Color-mostly Black People-Government Entities that are seemingly unwilling to work together, to pass legislation to make change that benefits everyone and not just a select-a.k.a. wealthy 1%-few. Unwillingness to address Climate Change inflicted by human activity on the Planet. Criminal Justice Reform that is truly Real for <u>All Classes of Citizens,</u> and not just a few. All this mess, because of The Father of Lies!

## 20.

The god of This World.

There's a reason why Satan has that unfortunate title. It is because of Adam's disobedience with regard to the forbidden fruit, way back in the Garden of Eden. Human Beings were supposed to be THE Caretakers of this planet in all aspects. Had Adam obeyed, I believe, no doubt, the Devil would have tried with someone else again and again. As it stands though; Adam failed the rest of Us, and now, control of this planet is under Satan.

Understand something okay? The Devil DOESN'T OWN the Earth as he'd like you and I to believe. Psalm 24: Vs. 1. "The Earth IS THE LORD'S, and all its fullness. The World, and those who dwell therein." Satan only has powerful influence as he roams all over the planet like a roaring lion, seeking whom he may devour. He seeks to disrupt Human History according to Scripture, so he can gain an edge over Our Lord and Savior...but he cannot, and never will. He's the direct reason that things are happening as they currently are in the world. Most particularly-and I'm just as guilty as anyone else in this mind you-'The Works of The Flesh' according to the Apostle Paul in Galatians Chapter 5: Vs. 19-21. Vs. 19. "Now, the works of the Flesh are evident which are: Adultery, Fornication, Uncleanness, Lewdness." Vs. 20. "Idolatry, Sorcery, Hatred, Contentions, Jealousies, Outbursts of Wrath, Selfish Ambitions, Dissentions, Heresies, Vs. 21. Envy, Murders, Drunkenness, Revelries, and the like of which I tell you beforehand, just as I also told you in time past that, those who practice such things <u>Will Not</u> Inherit the Kingdom of God!" I'd

## The Real Enemy Of All Mankind

been an Adulterer; Fornicator, Practitioner of Lewdness, Idolatry, Attempts at Sorcery in a time long ago, I'd expressed Hatred against other people, and been involved in Contentious Arguments over essentially nothing from time to time...I can just about cover all of those 'Works of The Flesh' just in my own life, and I openly admit it. Today however; I try not to practice any of these things anymore. I have to pray daily to stay 'Suited Up', so I don't. Still; there are times I fall short, and will continue to do so I'm afraid, because of this fleshly body I'm in, with the fleshly mind I carry in my head. It is these reasons in my opinion, that entire families today are falling apart like never before. That governments won't function as they're intended to. That the planet seems like it is on the brink of Nuclear War. That weather patterns are changing in ways we've never seen before, and etc. Satan's influence has a sure end on the way.

Perry Alan Pickens

## 21.

When Jesus went to Golgotha-the Place of a Skull-at Calvary, He knew full well what was yet to come: He'd been beaten, spat on, scorned, abused, more marred than any man, had stripes of His open flesh on his back ripped open by a Cat-O-Nine Tails, and a crown of thorns pressed down on His head. When He and the Soldiers that drove Him, arrived at Golgotha, they nailed His Hands and Feet-NAILED THEM-to the Cross. Man, that HAD to hurt! They picked up the Cross and hung him between two thieves. The abuse didn't end there either. Some Idiot Soldier had the idea of spearing Him in the side. More Blood and Water came out of Him. I mean, how much more could The God/Man, lose? To top it all off; one of the thieves mocked Him, and taunted Him. Asking why He couldn't save Himself? The other however; merely asked Him to remember him when He entered His Kingdom. Jesus told the guy on that very same day he would be with Him, in Paradise! The First Saint, to have asked for mercy and forgiveness, was a Thief. As Jesus hung on that Cross; I can imagine Him, thinking about all of the Human Beings living at that time, and everyone yet to be born afterward. To be sure; He very well could have called out to His Heavenly Father to send Legions of Angels to His Rescue, and get Him down off of that Cross. Yet, He didn't. You see, He looked down through the Annals of Time and saw a guy named Perry Alan Pickens. Saw his entire life, and the sins and crimes he'd commit. Jesus Loved Perry so much; that He endured the Cross, the Pain, the Blood Loss, the Spear Piercing...just so that Perry could also have an opportunity to have Life Eternal with Him. He died the death that Perry SHOULD HAVE. Took the punishment that Perry SHOULD HAVE. Then; Jesus TOOK EVERY SIN of Perry's and Nailed ALL OF THEM, right along with Himself, on that same Cross! When He Died, and after He was put in the grave, I can see Satan now: "I Got Him. At long last. I Got Him." That was short lived, because Jesus invaded Hell itself, fought to free every Imprisoned Soul, snatched The Keys of Hell AND Death from the Devil, and I can imagine the rest of The Story:

First Day: Satan; "Hey Death, you got Him. Right?" Death; "Yeah, I Got Him." Second Day: Satan; "Hey Death, you still Got Him. Right?" Death; "Don't worry Boss. Yeah, I Still Got Him." Third Day: All of Hell was recovering from the wounds that Our Lord inflicted on them all, when He took the keys of Hell and Death from Satan and then Got Up Out of The Grave...Forever! God-2. Satan-0!

Perry Alan Pickens

# Part III.

# Defeated Forever!

Perry Alan Pickens

## 22.

The Last Days.

Jesus said it Himself. Matthew 24: 36-44.

Vs. "But of that day and hour no one knows, not even the angels of heaven, but My Father only." Vs. 37. "But as the days of Noah were, so also will the coming of the Son of Man be." Vs. 38. "For as in the days before the flood, they were eating and drinking, marrying and giving in marriage, until the day that Noah entered the Ark." Vs. 39. "And did not know until the flood came and took them all away, so also will the coming of the Son of Man be." Vs. 40. "Then two men will be in the field; one will be taken, and the other left." Vs. 41. "Two women will be grinding at the mill; one will be taken, and the other left." Vs. 42. "Watch therefore, for you do not know what hour your Lord is coming." Vs. 43. "But know this, that if the master of the house had known what hour the thief would come, he would have watched and not allowed his house to be broken into." Vs. 44. "Therefore, you also be ready, for the Son of Man is coming at an hour you do not expect."

Time and again; people have debated over just exactly when Jesus will return to earth for his Church-The Saints-and even today, there's widespread disagreement even among Learned Biblical Scholars as to the meaning of the timing of His return as well. What many people continually fail to grasp, are the events that signal when the time of His return is imminent. For that, we've got to go back into the Old Testament to the Book of Daniel for the prophecy concerning what is known as: 'The Abomination of

Desolation'. Chapter 11: Vs. 31. "And forces shall be mustered by him, and they shall defile the sanctuary fortress, then they shall take away the daily sacrifices, and place there The Abomination of Desolation." Now, such a thing has already happened once in the month of December 168 B.C. by a fellow named Antiochus IV, but that isn't going to be THE Abomination yet to come. Now to be sure, there's one yet to come with Antichrist involved in that episode. Consider the Apostle Paul in 2nd Thessalonians Chapter 2: Vs. 1-12. Vs. 1. "Now, brethren concerning the coming of our Lord Jesus Christ and our gathering together to Him, we ask you." Vs. 2. "Not to be soon shaken in mind or troubled either by spirit or by word or by letter, as if from us, as though the day of Christ had come." Vs. 3. "Let no one deceive you by any means; for that day WILL NOT COME, until The Falling Away comes first, and the man of sin is revealed, the son of perdition."

23.

Vs. 4. "Who opposes and exalts himself above all that is called God or that is worshipped, so that he sits as God in the temple of God, showing himself that he is God." Vs. 5. "Do you not remember that when I was still with you, I told you these things?" Vs. 6. "And now you know what is restraining, that he may be revealed in his own time." Vs. 7. "For the mystery of lawlessness is already at work; only He who now restrains will do so until He is taken out of the way." Vs. 8. "And then the lawless one will be revealed whom the Lord will consume with the breath of His mouth and destroy with the brightness of His coming." Vs. 9. "The coming of the lawless one is according to the working of Satan, with all power, signs, and LYING

WONDERS." Vs. 10. And with all unrighteous deception among those who perish, because they did not receive the love of the truth, that they might be saved. Vs. 11. "And for this reason, God will send them strong delusion, that they should believe the lie." Vs. 12. "That they all may be condemned who did not believe the truth, but had pleasure in unrighteousness!" Wow!

    I'll try to make this as simple as I can. I believe 'the Lawless One', is a reference to, the Antichrist. As Christ Himself worked True and Divine Miracles, the Lawless One will work Fraudulent, Lying Wonders. He'll be the guy that actually will have the audacity to commit 'The Abomination of Desolation', by setting himself up as God!

    Everything that is currently going on today in Television for example, would NEVER have gone on 20-30 years ago. Sex is rampant

## The Real Enemy Of All Mankind

everywhere. 'Alternative Lifestyles'-LGBTQ-and the rights of people living in said lifestyles, are being recognized more and more by the Courts that never would have many years ago. Corruption by Elected Officials in just about any capacity, is a seeming common thing nowadays, and once would have been considered unheard of or shocking to say the least. Today's Children-and this is REALLY BAD-do not get punished like I used to when I was coming up, because now it is an actual crime to spank your youngster for whatever wrong he or she had done. I've even heard of kids taking their own Parents to Court, and Suing them...and winning, just for that alone! Consider the Wisest King who ever lived: King Solomon when he wrote in Proverbs 13: Vs. 24. "He who spares his rod, hates his Son. But he who Loves him, disciplines him promptly!"

Perry Alan Pickens

## The Real Enemy Of All Mankind

## 24.

I can hear it now: "So you think it is okay to beat your kids when they do wrong eh? Well, you deserve to be beaten too." Look: Whenever I got punished as a child and early teenager, it was because I did or said something that warranted BEING PUNISHED, in order for me to be corrected. It was not out of hate that my parents punished me. It was because of Love, because they wanted me to say and do what was right. Well, it had become evident that I had to get 'Whipped' some more as an older teenager and then young adult, and even after, by the Courts. Evidently, I didn't get the 'Get Right' Memo when I should have. The Judicial System has a way of 'Whipping' you when you have to appear in front of a Judge in a

Courtroom, and I've had my share. Doing Time in and of itself, DOES WHIP YOU. Your life ends up being changed in ways you wish it never had. I know, because I'm still getting the aftereffects even to this day!

Yet; in all of this, I must say that I'm Glad in a rather strange way, that the Lord had to use the Judicial System like He did, to get my attention to get me back on the path to Life instead of the path to certain Death. This shows me that, He Loves Me enough, to use the System to straighten me out. Now mind you, it took more than once, but I finally got the: 'Get Right' Memo!

Things are getting worse and worse these days. You would think that, in a country like the United States of America, supposedly the Wealthiest Country on the Planet, that NO ONE should be Homeless or Starving right? Yet we hear stories every day about people who experience suffering just like this. There are literally hundreds of thousands of Millionaires and Billionaires in this country and yet, perhaps one or two in a thousand, will actually use a good portion of their wealth to reach out to help others in need. The Lord does NOT like this kind of treatment by Wealthy People with regard to the Poor, for that is a sure sign of Greed and Pride.

Even established Charity Organizations such as: The Salvation Army, and others like it or similar to it, are seeing much less and less contributions now more than ever these days. Morality as a whole, has broken down to the point that-as I've alluded to before-wrong is right and right is wrong! These and a slew of other things only suggest that Satan's influence all over the planet, is increasing more and more...because he knows what's coming next!

I strongly urge you to pay attention as well.

Perry Alan Pickens

## 25.

The Last War/ Judgement!

For this Chapter; we go directly to The Revelator himself. The Disciple that Jesus Loved. John. Now; there had come a point in time in John's life, that he was sent to an Island known as Patmos, and essentially marooned there for helping to spread The Gospel. Yet, the Lord hadn't forgotten about him. The Lord came to John; on the Lord's Day, Sunday, the Christian Day of worship celebrating Jesus' Resurrection from the Dead I believe. John is tasked with writing a letter to the Seven Churches, in the region of what was known as Asia Minor. Revelation Chapter 1: Vs. 10-11. "I was in the Spirit on the Lord's Day, and I heard behind me a loud voice as of a trumpet." Vs. 11. "Saying: 'I AM the Alpha and the Omega, the First and the Last' and 'What you see, write in a book and send it to the Seven Churches which are in Ephesus, to Smyrna, to Pergamos, to Thyatira, to Sardis, to Philadelphia, and to Laodicea.' John turns around to see who it is speaking to him, and says this next in Vs. 12-16. Vs. 12. "Then I turned to see the voice that spoke with me. And having turned, I saw seven golden lampstands." Vs. 13. And in the midst of the seven lampstands, one like the Son of Man, clothed with a garment down to the feet and girded about the chest with a golden band." Vs. 14. "His head and hair were white like wool, as white as snow, and His eyes like a flame of fire." Vs. 15. "His feet were like fine brass, as if refined in a furnace, and His voice as the sound of many waters." Vs. 16. "He had in His right hand seven stars, out of His mouth went a sharp two-edged sword, and His countenance was like the sun shining in its strength." That, I can only imagine, would have certainly terrified me. Then see what happens next in Vs. 17-20.

Vs. 17." And, when I saw Him, I feel at His feet as dead. But He laid His right hand on me saying to me. 'Do not be afraid; I AM the First and the Last." Vs. 18. 'I AM He who lives and was dead, and behold I AM alive forevermore Amen. And I have the keys of Hades-Hell-and of Death.' Vs. 19. 'Write the things which you have seen, and the things which are, and the things which will take place after this.' Vs. 20. 'The mystery of the seven stars which you saw in My right hand, and the seven golden lampstands: The seven stars are the angels of the seven churches and the seven lampstands which you saw are the seven churches.'

Perry Alan Pickens

26.

Of the Seven Churches back then, only two had no criticism of any kind from the Lord. Smyrna's Commendation rather; was that they gracefully bear the sufferings they were enduring at the time. Many of them were being persecuted and thrown into prison. The Lord assures them to be faithful until death, and they will receive the Crown of Life. Philadelphia; the other Church, is commended for keeping the Faith and continuing to honor the Name of Jesus. Their reward will be to have a place in the presence of God, a New Name, and the name of the New Jerusalem, which will come directly from out of Heaven!

After that; several events will literally rock the planet, and

Judgements of varying kinds will occur. Many people will be Conquered. The First of Seven Seals. The Second: Great Conflict on Earth. If you're tired of hearing "No Justice. No Peace." Just wait. When the Second Seal hits, there will literally BE NO PEACE ANYWHERE! People WILL kill one another. Seal Number Three will be like a Famine as never before experienced. Prices ON EVERYTHING, will rise. Seal Number Four will be Death on a scale unlike what has ever happened before in the entire history of the planet. Man, and Beast alike, will suffer because over a fourth will die. The Fifth Seal is a promise from the Lord, that those who had suffered and died for His Name, would soon be joined by more in the same manner, and then Vengeance from the Lord Himself. Seal Six; reveals mighty occurrences in the sky and on the planet's surface. A Great Earthquake. A Darkened Sun. A Blood Moon. These and other events will literally cause people to run and hide in the mountains hoping for death by Avalanche or Rock Slides. I wonder why? What or Whom will they try hiding from? I doubt they'll escape anyway. Seal Seven literally will be the Sealing of 144,000 of the Remnants of the Original Twelve Tribes. To be sure, Gentile Saints; Non-Jewish, are also included. Just not in the same number. So, The Sealed suggests there will be much, much more.

I digress however. Now, to get to the main thrust of this chapter. Revelation 19: Vs. 11-21. Rather than going verse by verse as I previously had, I'll give you a Play-By-Play. Jesus comes down out of Heaven with THE Angelic Army behind Him, coming to do battle with The Beast-Antichrist-and his army on the earth. Yeah, The Beast had literally shown up first in Chapter 13 and gave people that worshipped him, a Mark on the Right Hand or Forehead. Warning: DON'T TAKE THE 666 MARK!

## 27.

When Jesus was on earth the first time, the Devil tried tempting Him three times. The Third Temptation was that he'd give the Lord All the Kingdoms of the earth, for they had been under his control. Jesus refused by using the Word of God, in all three temptations. Now, Jesus is back and the Game has changed. Satan sends out the Beast to fight with the Lord-the Coward can't do it himself-and the Beast has every armed force on earth and every weapon of all kinds utilized to try defeating Christ. Bad Move.

This is where it gets ugly. Jesus literally blasts with power from His very mouth, those aligned against Him, and the birds of the air WILL have a Feast Like No Other, feeding on the flesh of dead Satanic Aligned Soldiers. It isn't over though. The Beast and The False Prophet-the Lying Wonders Guy- will be captured and thrown into the Lake of Fire burning with Brimstone.

Then, Satan himself will be caught, bound and thrown into the bottomless pit for a thousand years. If you're in the number of the Saints- and I pray I am too-that will reign with Christ during that time, you're literally Good-To-Go Forever. Revelation 20: Vs. 4-6. "And I saw thrones and they sat on them, and judgement was committed to them. Then I saw the souls of those who had been beheaded for their witness to Jesus and for the Word of God, who had not worshipped the Beast or his image, and had not received his mark on their foreheads or on their hands. And they lived and reigned with Christ for a thousand years." Vs. 5. "But the rest of the dead did not live again, until the thousand years were finished-pay attention to this part-This Is, The First Resurrection." Vs. 6. "Blessed and holy is he who has part in the First Resurrection. Over such, the second death has no power, but they shall be Priests of God and of Christ, and shall reign with Him a thousand years." You might think again, that Satan should have given up at this point. No. Remember, he's Hard-Headed. After the thousand years, the Devil will try one final time, to gather as many forces as he can, to attack the camp of the Saints and the Beloved City. God Himself, now shows up and Shows Out. Blasting everyone and thing that tries attacking the Saints, and now Satan is again captured, but THIS TIME, he himself is thrown into the lake of fire and brimstone right along with the Beast and False Prophet...to be Tormented Day and Night. Forever, and ever! Revelation Chapter 20: Vs. 7-10.

Perry Alan Pickens

God-3. Satan-Goose Egg. Zip. Zero. For Good!

## 28.

Judgement!

I can assure you of this. THIS JUDGEMENT, will be the End-All-TO-It-All. Revelation 20: Vs. 11-15. Vs. 11. "Then I saw a great white throne and Him who sat on it, from whose face the earth and the heaven fled away. And there was found no place for them." Vs. 12. "And I saw the dead, small and great, standing before God, and books were opened and another book was opened, which is the Book of Life. And the dead were judged according to their works, by the things which were written in the books." Vs. 13. "The Sea gave up the dead who were in it, and Death and Hades delivered up the dead who were in them. And they were judged, each one, according to his works."

Vs. 14. "Then, Death and Hades were cast into the Lake of Fire. This Is, The Second Death." Vs. 15. "And, ANYONE, not found written in the Book of Life, was cast into the Lake of Fire."

God keeps a record of everything we say; think, and do in this life. He must have literally Billions of Books on everyone, and I'm certain He has one on Me too. Recall however; that Jesus-now-is a Mediator between the Father and me. The Scripture tells me that if I mess up-sin-Jesus is faithful and just to forgive me of sin and cleanse me from all unrighteousness. There's even a Sea of Forgetfulness, that God casts My Sins and Crimes into every time I Repent of any wrong, I know I've done. Micah. Chapter 7: Vs. 18-20.

The point in all of this is: You nor I, DO NOT want to be a part of the Great White Throne Judgement.

## The Real Enemy Of All Mankind

That will be reserved for everyone that has rejected Jesus as Lord and Savior, and by the way they lived their lives. It doesn't matter what kind of Education you had. How much Wealth you acquired, no matter what kind of Good, you think warrants you getting into Heaven, if it isn't by the Blood of Jesus Christ and accepting Him as Lord and Savior? Forget it. NOTHING you or I could ever do or have done, outside of accepting God's Free Gift of Salvation through Jesus, will get you into Heaven to stay. ALL HAVE SINNED, AND FALLEN SHORT OF THE GLORY OF GOD! It doesn't get any simpler than that. Satan has been and will be Defeated Permanently. To be sure; there's going to be a period of time I'm equally certain, to be tried in, regarding the Shape of Things to Come.

I hope and pray, I make it through all the way to The End!

I hope and pray the same, For You too!!

## 29.

## A Final Word.

Today's Media: Social-Media, Internet, TV, Magazines, Newspapers, Radio, and all the devices used to access all of these Media, are Tools. They are tools for Satan's use, but also for God's use as well. You see, it all comes down to which way you choose to go.

Note that I said; which way YOU CHOOSE to go.

You can choose to totally ignore everything written in this book about Our Common Enemy. Just go ahead and fill your mind with all the stuff out there in all of today's Media, that The Devil has, continues to, AND WILL continue to throw at you so that you forget all about The Lord. Or.

You can choose to seriously consider everything in this book, and take a good look within yourself. See if there's anything you know deep-down, that you know needs to be changed within you...before you become like the rest of today's declining world. You see it all the time on the News: Violence, Shootings, Kidnappings, Corruption in practically ALL LEVELS of Society these days and I could go on and on and on. You should have gotten the gist of it long before now I trust.

Satan...is The Source of it all! And there's only One Solution to him:

Jesus Christ. The Savior of All Mankind!

## The Real Enemy Of All Mankind

Read God's Word for yourself if you don't believe me. In fact, DON'T take my word for it. TAKE GOD'S WORD FOR IT. Because believe me, the day WILL COME, when you wish you had...if you don't believe me now. The Day I'm referring to of course will be THE DAY OF JUDGEMENT. The Judge will be Almighty God Himself, and if you've ever faced a Judge on earth-as I have-none will be as terrifying as facing HIM!

And HIS JUDGEMENT? That Verdict-unless you accept Jesus Christ as Lord and Savior and live for Him-will be the one you'll regret hearing FOR ALL ETERNITY!

Perry Alan Pickens

## 30.

Last Call and Choice.

There it is. Now you know who is really out to ensure your Eternal Destruction. You also know how to avoid it. I have given you the Truth of the only one who can and will save you from Hell, and He is Jesus Christ. He Lives, and is alive forevermore. He cannot ever die again. He has accomplished the Mission His Heavenly Father sent Him to do, and will finish the rest of Human History before long. His Return IS A CERTAINTY. The Question you have to answer for yourself is this:

Where am I going after I die? I know where I'm going: Heaven! The reason I know for certain is found in Romans Chapter 10: Vs. 9-12. You can read it for yourself. Now, at the beginning of this book, I gave you the Sinner's Prayer to Pray to receive the Free Gift of God's Salvation through Jesus Christ's shed Blood, and His Rising from the Dead. I have done what I have long believed the Holy Spirit wanted me to do...which was to write this particular book. According to the message of Ezekiel Chapter 33, I have done the work the Lord wanted me to do. If you have finished this entire book-and I pray you have-then I am relieved of whatever decision you make from this point on. If you accept Christ, your blood won't be on My Hands. If you don't, your blood is on your own head. You, have been warned! Now I'm going to finish with this Prayer:

"Holy Father; I first and foremost ask for forgiveness of any and all sins I've committed in thought, word, and deed. I ask for You to cleanse me from all unrighteousness. I have finished the task You set before me, with regard to this book You told me to write. I have given the Truth of the Enemy to everyone that now reads this book, and pray that, this book leads the reader to Your Holy Word, to find Salvation through Your Holy Son Jesus Christ. Father; I pray for Divine Protection from those who will attack me by criticism or by any other means, and to remain steadfast in the decision to have written and have published this book, because it is according to Your Will that I have written it. Bless everyone who reads it, and call whomever You Will, to Salvation through Your Holy Son Jesus Christ. Glorify Yourself Oh Heavenly Father. For the Might, the Power, and the Glory are always and always will be Yours and Yours Alone Oh God. I Seal This Prayer, in the Name of Jesus. Amen!"

Finis.

www.ingramcontent.com/pod-product-compliance
Lightning Source LLC
Chambersburg PA
CBHW071454070526
44578CB00001B/333